I Have Called You By Name

by
Sister Jean Helen Langton, CSJ

Illustrated by
Daughters of St. Paul

ST. PAUL EDITIONS

NIHIL OBSTAT:
    Rev. Richard V. Lawlor, S.J.
    Censor

IMPRIMATUR:
    ✢ Bernard Cardinal Law
    Archbishop of Boston

This updated edition was originally published by the Gregorian Institute of America.

ISBN 0-8198-3614-1

Copyright © 1986, by the Daughters of St. Paul

Printed in the U.S.A., by the Daughters of St. Paul
50 St. Paul's Ave., Boston, MA 02130

The Daughters of St. Paul are an international Congregation of women religious serving the Church with the communications media.

CONTENTS

To the Reader ———————————— 7
Our Mother Mary ———————————— 9
Saint Thomas the Apostle ——————— 13
Saint John the Evangelist ——————— 19
Saint Denis ———————————————— 23
Saint Agnes ——————————————— 27
Saint Patrick, Bishop of Ireland ——— 33
Saint Elizabeth of Hungary ————— 37
Saint Therese of Lisieux ——————— 41

Theme of Book:

The theme of *I Have Called You By Name* is an attempt to awaken in children the extraordinary adventure their lives can be. God has called each of them into being. There are no two persons alike. The saints whose heroic lives are written in this book were ordinary people. Because they listened to the call of God, their lives were almost-unbelievably exciting, courageous, and joyous.

This book, written in an attractive style, appeals to young children. Sanctity becomes understandable. Based on historical fact, ancient legends and traditions, the major incidents in these stories convey a deep sense of conviction that all of us, without exception, are called to sanctity.

The Author:

Sister Jean Helen Langton, CSJ, is a native New Yorker. Her birthplace was on the site where Lincoln Center Plaza is presently located.

Sister is a member of the Congregation of the Sisters of St. Joseph of Brentwood, New York. She has spent many years as an educator in the Diocese of Brooklyn. Being Directress of a Primary Learning Center in St. Athanasius School was the most challenging and rewarding of her teaching experiences. Sister is now in the Maria Regina Convent, Brentwood, N.Y. 11717.

I HAVE CALLED YOU BY NAME; YOU ARE MINE
(Is. 43)

To The Reader:

When you were born, your loving parents chose your name.

It was not easy to do. Your coming was such a special event that choosing a name for you was a very important decision to make.

God had already called you by name. It was because of His great love for you that you were called into being in the first place.

In this book, you will read about some fascinating people. They answered God's call in a very unique way. Their lives were full of exciting incidents. Enriched, as you are, with a loving relationship with God, they had the courage to face life's experiences with joyous enthusiasm.

Ask God to help you. Then, like these saints, everyone you come in contact with will be better and happier because of you.

Our Mother Mary

Far across the sea in the country of Palestine there is a little village nestled among the hills. It is called Nazareth. Many, many years ago there lived in Nazareth the most beautiful girl in all the world. Her name was Mary. She was holy and pure. She was kind and considerate. Everyone loved Mary.

Joseph was the village carpenter, and he loved Mary very much. Joseph was honest and good. Mary had promised to marry him.

You see, God had chosen Mary to be the Mother of His Son, Jesus. God had chosen Joseph to be Jesus' foster father. But Mary and Joseph did not know God's wonderful plan for them. Don't you just love a surprise? No one in the world ever had such a wonderful surprise as Mary had!

One evening, Mary was kneeling in prayer. Mary prayed that God would soon send someone to earth to save the people from their sins. She knew that many people were sad and lonely.

Suddenly, a very bright light filled the room! Looking up, Mary saw a young man in a white robe. His face was radiantly bright!

It was the Angel Gabriel. He was God's messenger. "Hail, full of grace, the Lord is with you. Blessed are you among women," said the angel. Mary was frightened! "Fear not, Mary," said the angel. Then he told her the most wonderful news!

He told her that she was going to be the Mother of Jesus. Mary was so happy! She was no longer afraid. She told the angel she would do whatever God wanted. Mary knew that God would take care of everything. A short time later the angel told the good news to Joseph in a dream. Soon after, Mary and Joseph were married.

Mary loved to keep house for Joseph. She cooked his meals. While they ate, they often talked about Jesus' coming. How they longed to see Him! They could hardly wait!

Everyone knows the story of the first Christmas, and how happy it made the world. You have heard how the innkeeper said, "No room." Mary and Joseph were turned away. Finally, they found a little stable on the hillside. Then Jesus was born. A glorious star shone in the sky. The shepherds heard the angels' song, and they went to find Jesus.

Wise men came from the East to adore Him. Jesus was so beautiful! He was the most beautiful Baby the world had ever seen. He was God!

He came from heaven and became a Baby to show us how to live. Mary held Jesus in her arms; Joseph watched over them and kept them from harm.

There lived in those days a very wicked king named Herod. He heard that Jesus was born, and that He was the great King of heaven and earth. Herod was very angry. He said, "I will find the Baby and kill Him! He will never take my throne!"

Sending his soldiers to Bethlehem, he ordered, "Go and kill all the baby boys under two years of age! This Baby they call the King, shall die!"

But God was watching over the Holy Family. He sent an angel to warn Joseph. "Arise, Joseph, and take the Child and His Mother and go into Egypt. Stay there until I shall tell you to return."

Joseph did as the angel directed. Although leaving their little home saddened them, Mary and Joseph trusted in their loving Father.

In due time, the angel came again. "King Herod is dead," he said. "Now you may go home."

It was wonderful to be in Nazareth again! Their friends and relatives were so glad to see Mary and Joseph!

They had never seen Jesus before. He was such a good, loving Child that all the other children in the village liked to be with

Him. He played games with them. Jesus also taught them how to cherish their parents by His example.

Mary knew that Jesus would have to leave their little home some day. He had come to save the world.

When Jesus began to go from village to village preaching to the people, Mary often followed Him with the crowd. She watched Him heal the sick. She watched Him give sight to the blind. One day she saw Him raise a young man from death to life. She listened to His stories, which were called parables.

Oh, how sad she was when she saw that wicked men hated Him because He was so good! Some of them plotted to kill Him. One night they sent soldiers to capture Him. These evil men told lies about Jesus. They crowned Him with thorns and called Him bad names.

Jesus did not complain. He wanted to suffer and die to save men. Mary stayed close to her Son. She wished, when they nailed Jesus to the Cross, that they would kill her instead of Him.

Mother Mary was sad and lonely after Jesus died. But she remembered that He had said He would return.

Then, on Easter Sunday morning, He arose from the tomb all bright and beautiful. How joyful Mary was!

Jesus stayed on earth a little while longer. Then, one day while His Mother, His Apostles, and a large crowd of people watched, Jesus went back to heaven. The clouds hid Him from their sight.

Mary stayed with the Apostle John. Some of the other Apostles went to far off lands to tell people about Jesus. Whenever they came back, Mary was there to care for them.

At last, the nicest day of all came for our Mother! Jesus took her to heaven. There He crowned her Queen of heaven and earth.

How happy Jesus was! The angels and saints sang and rejoiced. They loved their beautiful Queen.

So you see, Mary is your Queen also. She will always guard and protect you. She is so kind and gentle. No other queen was ever like her! What an honor to be a child of such a Mother! You will never know, until you go home to heaven yourself, how much Mary, your Mother, loves you.

Do you show your love for her? The best way you can do that is to love her Son, Jesus, all of your life.

Saint Thomas the Apostle

Don't you just hate it when you tell people something really important and they say, "I don't believe it!" They don't even give you a chance to explain. Well, there are some boys and girls like that, you know.

You just say to them, "Wow! You should see my new rocket ship go!"

"I don't believe it!" they'll interrupt, even before you say, "It's a plastic model."

Or, after school, you can hardly wait to tell your best friend, Susan, about that star you got for spelling. "Seeing is believing!" she'll answer. This can really be a problem.

Many years ago, there was a man named Thomas, who was one of our Lord's Apostles. Thomas was an agreeable fellow, but he had a terrible habit of saying, "I don't believe it!"

On the first Easter Sunday night, something wonderful happened! The Blessed Mother and the Apostles were so happy! Jesus had just appeared to them. All of a sudden, He just stood there in the room with them. They were so glad to see Him! Thomas was the only Apostle not there at that time.

You can imagine how excited the other Apostles were when Thomas arrived. They all talked at once. "Jesus was here! We saw Him! We saw Him!"

And can you guess what Thomas said? "I will not believe it, until I see Him myself!"

Well, Jesus must have been very patient with Thomas, because one week later, He came back again. This time, Thomas was there. Jesus said, "Come, Thomas, see my wounds; it is I."

Poor Thomas! He took a few steps forward. Then he fell on his knees. Looking up into our Lord's face, he cried out, "My Lord and my God!"

Wouldn't you think Thomas would believe anything after that? Well, he didn't!

When Jesus sent the Holy Spirit upon the Apostles, they began to preach. Later, Peter, who was the leader, sent each Apostle into a different country to tell the people about the one, true God.

It just happened that Thomas was chosen to go to India and here are some of the stories told about him:

"I don't believe I'll ever learn how to speak the language of those people," he said. However, he was so happy to be going some place where he could tell people about Jesus, that he didn't worry too much about that.

On the first Pentecost Sunday, thousands of people understood Peter's sermon even though he wasn't speaking their language. God would also see to it that Thomas would be understood by the people of India.

Thomas traveled with a servant of an Indian king. During the voyage, they landed at a certain port. A wedding feast was going on in the village. Because Thomas was traveling with the king's servant, he was invited. There was a girl there who was playing the flute. Thomas began to sing. The dancing stopped suddenly. Everyone listened to Thomas. They couldn't understand him, but the flute girl did. Thomas sang about Jesus' miracles, His love, and His message to us. He had never sung in that way before.

"I will sing that song all my life," the flute girl promised as Thomas was leaving the village that night.

That promise made Thomas very happy. "What a nice way to tell people about Jesus!" he thought.

Finally, after a long journey, they arrived in India.

The king, Gundafor, sent for Thomas immediately. "What can you do besides sing?" he asked.

"Oh! I'm a good carpenter," said Thomas. "I can also make plows, and oars for boats, and lots of things. I'm also very good at building palaces for kings." Thomas wasn't speaking of an earthly palace, though.

King Gundafor was delighted! He needed a new palace. His old one was badly in need of repair. "Besides," he thought, "a king should have more than one palace."

So he began to give orders and make plans. "Make my palace of beautiful white marble," he commanded. "I want doors toward the east for light. Put windows toward the west for air. And don't forget the gardens and the fountains. I want the best palace you can build! You just ask my steward for money as you need it. Spare no expense."

"Right, Your Majesty," said Thomas, "you shall have it! No king will ever have a more beautiful palace than yours."

So the king ordered his steward to give Thomas a great sum of money to buy the marble, the stone, and the gold trimmings.

"O King," said Thomas, "haven't you noticed that many of your subjects are very poor? They don't have enough to eat. With this money we can supply all of them with food and clothing for a long time to come. Your subjects will be so grateful, that they will love you as no other king has ever been loved. You will get a great reward when you go to heaven!"

The king thought it over. "All right, Thomas, give the money to them, and I'll supply more for my palace. What kind of reward will I get in heaven?"

"Oh, never mind that now," said Thomas, "that will be a big surprise!"

So Thomas went about the streets of India giving away the king's money to the poor. Then he bought materials for rebuilding houses. The poor people were astounded at their good fortune.

While all this was going on, Thomas always had a large crowd following him. This was his chance to tell the people about Jesus.

Then one day, Thomas again arrived at the palace. King Gundafor was really getting impatient. "Well, it's about time," he said. "When are you going to start building my palace?"

"Don't worry, Your Majesty," said Thomas, "I'm building it. I need more money, though, much more. The poor people have all been taken care of, but do you know that you have many sick people in your kingdom? They have no medicine; they have no one to take care of them. Worst of all, there isn't even one hospital for them to go to. Let me use this money to build one. Your subjects will love you more than ever, and God will reward you in heaven."

"I'm getting tired of waiting, Thomas, but go ahead and give them their medicine and their hospital. This is the first time I've ever heard of a king having to wait until last. But, have it your way. Just don't forget about my palace. And Thomas, I think it would be nice if you put solid gold bars on the doors, don't you?"

"Don't you worry, King Gundafor, your palace will be more beautiful than any you have ever dreamed of. I promise you that." Thomas went off to make plans to build the hospital.

Just about this time, the king's brother died suddenly. This made the king so unhappy that he became more impatient than ever.

"Well, at least I'll soon have a brand new palace to cheer me up," he thought. So he sent for Thomas and demanded, "When are you going to start building my palace?"

"Oh, I have been building it all these long months," said Thomas boldly. "You cannot see your palace now, O King, but you will see it when you die. All the good things I have done with your money will be your palace in heaven."

You can imagine how angry the king was! "Take him away!" roared the king. "Kill him!"

After Thomas was led away, the king stormed and raged. He paced up and down, murmuring to himself, "Palace in heaven! Who needs a palace in heaven?"

"Will you sell your palace to me, Gundafor?" said a familiar voice. The king almost collapsed with fright! Standing before him was his dead brother!

"Gundafor, listen to me! Your palace in heaven, made of good deeds to the sick and the poor, is more precious than the most beautiful palace on this earth." Then the brother disappeared.

"Go get Thomas out of the dungeon!" called the king to his servants. "Prepare a feast! This is the happiest day of my life!"

When Thomas was brought before the king, he was amazed. Of course, Thomas didn't know what had happened to change the king's mind about him.

But the biggest surprise came when the king said, "Thomas, I want to be baptized! I want my subjects to be Christians, too!"

Thomas caught himself just in time. You can guess what he had almost answered. Thomas had almost said, "I don't believe it!"

Saint John the Evangelist

When you go to school for the first time, or when you move to a new neighborhood, the first question everybody asks is, "What's your name?"

Do you know why this is so? Because the first step in knowing you is knowing your name.

As people come to know you better, your name means all the things that remind them of you. It reminds them of the color of your hair, your eyes, and your friendly smile. And most of all, it means, I hope, that you are nice to be with. You should be agreeable, especially if your name is John. There are many boys named John.

Do you know that when Jesus was on earth, He had a very good friend named John? John was one of Jesus' twelve Apostles.

This is how they met. One day John and his brother, James, were sitting in their father's fishing boat mending their nets. Fishing was lots of fun, but mending the nets wasn't so pleasant. Jesus came along the beach. He asked them if they'd like to be among His chosen followers. Would they like to! Why, they were all excited. Who wouldn't like to be chosen by Jesus? So they forgot all about their nets and their fishing boats, and they went along with Him. John was the youngest of the twelve men who were Jesus' Apostles.

John was chosen to go up to the mountain with Peter and James on that wonderful day when Jesus showed them that He was the Son of God.

John was standing at the foot of the cross when Jesus was dying.

Because he was so faithful, it was to John that Jesus gave the care of His Mother, Mary.

Like the other Apostles, John went about the countries of Asia Minor teaching the people about the one true God and His Son, Jesus Christ. He would tell them over and over how much God loved them. They were amazed to hear this, especially those who had led evil lives. When they heard that God loves even sinners, many of them became Christians. And now, here are some of the stories told about John:

One day when John was old he met a young man who wanted to be a Christian. He seemed to be so sincere that John took a special interest in him. He brought the young man to the bishop of that city and said, "I am going on a journey. I would like to entrust my young friend to you while I am away. When you have taught him all about the one true God, baptize and confirm him. He will be my trusted disciple when I return."

Some time later, John returned to the city. He went directly to the bishop's house.

"Alas," the bishop said sadly, "your friend has gone! While you were away, he got in with bad company and became a highway robber."

Although John was tired and weary, and very disappointed, he sent for a horse and a guide. Immediately he started off. Deeper and deeper he rode into the mountains.

Finally, after many days of searching, he found the robbers and among them his cherished friend.

When the young robber saw his good friend, John, he was very ashamed and ran away to hide.

John, who was on horseback, easily caught up with him.

"Why do you run from me, my boy?" he asked. "I am an old man and unarmed. I would give my life for you just as Jesus did."

Hearing this, the robber fell to the ground and sobbed as though his heart would break. Leaving his evil companions, he returned with John to the city. For many years, he was a faithful friend and helper.

In Rome at this time, there was a very cruel Emperor named Domitian. He hated all Christians. John was the only one of Jesus' Apostles who was still alive. All the others had been cruelly tortured, and put to death by evil men. They had died joyfully for Jesus; He had died for them.

Domitian decided that he would get rid of John also.

So many people loved John! Many of these people weren't Christians. But John was so gentle and kind that they listened to him as he told them about Jesus.

This made Domitian angry. He tried to think of a very cruel death for John. This wasn't hard for Domitian to do, because he was such a tyrant.

He ordered his soldiers to fill up a very large tank with oil. Then a fire was lighted and the tank was put over it. When the oil was boiling hot, Domitian gave the order, "Throw him in!" The rough soldiers grabbed John and threw him into the hot, bubbling oil.

You would never guess what happened next! The oil cooled just as John's body touched it. Instead of burning him, it was like a refreshing bath.

Domitian and the soldiers were terribly frightened! "It's a magic trick!" he shouted. "Take him away."

Now Domitian really had a problem! He wouldn't dare try to kill John after that miracle. He couldn't bear to have John around preaching about Jesus. He sent him away to the Island of Patmos.

There was no one on the island to preach to, but John didn't waste his time. He wrote about all the beautiful visions of heaven that he had seen.

After Domitian's death, John came back from exile. He was old and feeble, and could no longer travel. He wrote an account of all that he could remember about Jesus. There were so many wonderful memories! Now when you hear a story about Jesus' life on earth written by Saint John, you'll know why he is called "The Evangelist." An Evangelist is one who tells about Jesus.

John lived to be more than ninety years old. Each day he asked his faithful friends to carry him to the Temple steps. There the people would gather around him. He was too feeble to preach, so he would just say over and over, "My little children, love one another."

One day, someone in the crowd said, "John, why do you keep repeating the same thing over and over? Why don't you say something different?"

John smiled and answered gently, "Because, if you do this, you are keeping the Word of the Lord, 'My little children, love one another.'"

Now, if your name is John, you should be very proud of it.

Saint Denis

You must have noticed that one of the common names for boys is Denis. You have to admit, too, that it is a strong, manly name.

If your name is Denis, then you know how most people smile when they hear your name for the first time.

Don't they look at you in that, "Oh, so it's Denis, is it?" way. Of course, they are teasing you. Your name just reminds them of that funny little character in a cartoon book by the name of "Dennis the Menace."

They probably don't know you are named after a wonderful saint. Most of what we know about him comes from old legends.

Nothing very important is known about Denis as a little boy, except that he was born in Greece.

He also had a strange hobby for a boy. When other boys of his age were out playing games of war and the like, you'd never guess what Denis was doing. He was studying books and pictures of the stars and other planets. Then, at night, he used to tiptoe out of his room. He would go up to the roof and study the sky.

As Denis grew older, he met other boys who had the same hobby.

One day they were talking about tides and storms and things like that. "It must be the Greek gods who cause such things," said one of his friends.

All of these boys were pagans. These pagans didn't know about the one true God. They prayed to the sun god and the god of war. They had goddesses, too. Venus was the goddess of beauty. Artemis was the moon god.

Denis was beginning to notice things about these gods. He had often looked at their images in the temple. They didn't look to him as though they had much power. They were very big and ugly looking. People feared them.

"I don't believe our gods have any power," said Denis. "There must be a God we've never heard of who controls these wonderful powers of nature."

The other boys looked alarmed. What if a pagan leader heard Denis! They were terrified!

"Don't you know you could be killed for saying such things, Denis?" asked his friends.

But Denis was fearless. He just wanted to know the truth.

A few years later, there was an altar erected in the city of Athens. On it was carved the words, "To the Unknown God." The city was just full of statues and altars, so one more didn't make any difference.

Well, it just so happened that around this time a visitor came to the city. The visitor was Paul of Tarsus. Surely you've heard of Saint Paul.

He is the one who had hated Christians. One day he was riding to Damascus to make trouble for them.

A sudden flash of lightning threw Paul off his horse. He was struck blind! Later, he was healed by a Christian named Ananias.

After that, Paul knew better than to persecute Christians. In fact, he became one himself. Then he began to do the same thing he used to hate them for. He preached to the pagans about Jesus.

There was a hill in Athens called the Hill of Mars. It seemed to be a good place to hold meetings. Men who liked to make speeches used to get up there and talk.

One day Paul was invited to make a speech. He would have done it anyway. Paul was always preaching about Christ.

Paul had found a good starting point for his sermon. He had looked around at all the false gods. And he had seen the monument to the unknown god.

"Wouldn't you like to know about this one?" he asked. You can guess which one he meant, can't you? "Wouldn't you like to know about the 'Unknown God?'"

Denis was very interested in what Paul had to say.

"I knew it all the time," he said to his friends. "This man, Paul, speaks the truth. There is only one God!"

So Denis told Paul he would like to hear all about the God of the Christians.

Paul knew the whole story, because Jesus had died on the cross just a short time before Paul was converted to Christianity.

When he told Denis and the crowds about how Jesus had been crucified, and had risen from the dead, they looked at one another. They were amazed!

"This is wonderful!" some exclaimed.

Paul promised to stay with them a little while. He spent every day teaching them.

Denis was one of the first to become a Christian.

Later on, a wonderful thing happened. He was appointed Bishop of Athens.

He was such a good bishop that many of the pagans of Athens became Christians.

The years passed quickly. Then, one day Denis received a fearful message. A very cruel pagan leader had just become Emperor. This Emperor despised all Christians!

Some of Paul's most faithful followers were tortured because they wouldn't adore false gods.

The Emperor sent for Denis. "We will stop all this nonsense!" he shouted. "You have caused so much trouble among our people, that you shall die!"

Denis bravely replied, "I shall be happy to die in the service of the one true God, Jesus Christ."

This answer made the Emperor furious. "Take him away! Take him away!" he raged. "Burn him alive!"

The rough guards took Denis to the Hill of Mars. There he was burned alive.

Saint Paul was not in Athens at that time. Hearing the news of Denis' death, he was deeply saddened, but he praised God for having given him such a faithful friend.

Now, the next time someone asks your name, you just proudly say, "My name is Denis. Would you like to hear about my wonderful patron saint?"

Saint Agnes

Many, many years ago there lived in Rome, a very beautiful girl. Her name was Agnes, which means "lamb." Her parents were wealthy. Some of the legends about Agnes paint this picture of her:

Agnes was gentle and pure and sweet. She was twelve years of age at the time of our story. Girls of her age, who lived in those days, almost eighteen hundred years ago, were already like adults.

They had learned to cook, to weave, and to sew. They knew all about managing a home. It wasn't unusual for girls, even as young as Agnes was, to marry.

Agnes was so very beautiful that she didn't have to worry about being popular. When she was among her friends, all the boys of her age and older "just happened to be passing by."

Among these pagan boys, there were some who belonged to noble Roman families. How surprised they were to find that Agnes hardly noticed them. She wasn't the least bit concerned about popularity.

While some girls were saying, "Well, who does she think she is?" the boys were thinking up all kinds of ways to gain her attention. But they were wasting their time. Agnes wasn't interested.

Can you guess why? Well, I'll tell you. Agnes was a Christian. She had promised to give all her love to Jesus. It wouldn't have been sensible if she had made that promise and then married a pagan, would it? A pagan doesn't believe in God.

You know what happens when some people don't get their own way? One of these young men was so angry because Agnes

wouldn't promise to marry him, that he went to the governor of the city.

"That Agnes is a Christian," he said. "She will not adore the gods of Rome!"

That did it! The governor sent for Agnes immediately. He was furious, and he meant to show it. He was in for a big surprise!

When the soldiers brought Agnes into his palace, he just stared at her. "What a beautiful girl!" he finally exclaimed.

"Oh, come now, Agnes, why do you want to be one of those foolish Christians? All you have to do is offer incense to the gods of Rome."

The young man who had accused her, then tried all kinds of bribery to get her to marry him. "You will live in a magnificent palace of white marble. Wait till you see the beautiful jewelry you will wear as my bride." But to all this, Agnes had just one answer. "I prefer to serve the Lord Jesus Christ."

You can imagine how long the governor's patience lasted. He had never met such a determined child.

"I'll fix her!" he raged. Then he sent for his palace soldiers. "If we frighten her enough, she'll give up her silly notions," the governor said. "Go get the instruments of torture from the dungeon," he ordered.

In the meantime, big fires were lighted in the courtyard. Iron hooks, racks, and sharp instruments were brought in and thrown down near where Agnes was standing.

She looked at them, and wasn't the least bit frightened. In fact, she looked happy. "How wonderful it will be to die for Christ!" she said.

The crowds were astounded at her bravery. The governor, in a fury, then ordered her to be burned alive. This time he meant it!

Then the strangest thing happened. The flames shot out all around her and Agnes wasn't burned at all!

One of the young men in the crowd insulted Agnes. Immediately he fell to the ground, struck blind. His friends, terrified, begged Agnes to cure him. Bending over him, she gently touched his eyes, and his sight was restored. With a cry of thanks, he disappeared into the crowd.

While all this was going on, the governor was just about frightened out of his wits. He couldn't admit to the crowds that a girl had gotten the better of him, so he tried to hide his fear.

"Get a sword!" he commanded. When one was handed to him, he thrust it into the hand of the chief executioner.

"Well, what are you waiting for?" the governor roared. "Cut off her head!"

Trembling with fear, the murderer raised his hand, and, with one powerful blow, cut off Agnes' head.

Until the last moment of her life, Agnes prayed aloud.

Christians had no rights at all in pagan Rome. Even though Agnes was the only child of wealthy parents, it made no difference.

Her mother and father were very sad. They took their beloved child away and buried her in a tomb.

After that day so many people came to the tomb that a guard of soldiers had to be placed there. With swords and threats, they tried to keep people away, but there was just no use trying. More and more people came to visit Agnes' tomb.

So you see, Agnes was loved more than ever after her death.

Christians of those days certainly needed courage. They went to her tomb daily to pray for help. "If this girl could be so brave," they said, "surely, if we ask her, she will give us courage, too."

Whenever you see a statue or picture of Saint Agnes, you will notice something special about it. In her arms is a snowy white baby lamb. After hearing this story, you must know the reason for that. The little lamb is a symbol of purity.

Saint Agnes has a great love for all children. She is their special saint. If you are a boy, you will probably say, "Oh, she has no use for boys! Didn't she always ignore them?"

Well, you must remember that Agnes was a young Christian. In those days being a Christian was considered a terrible thing.

Most of the boys and girls Agnes knew were pagans. If anything went wrong, such as bad weather, which ruined the crops, whose fault was it? The pagans said, "Those awful Christians, of course!" If a fire broke out, the pagans said, "Those dreadful Christians must have started it!" The Christians were to blame for every evil event that happened. That's what the pagans claimed.

Now you understand why Agnes avoided pagan boys.

Saint Agnes' feast day is January 21st. Ask her to help you to always do what you know is right.

Saint Patrick, Bishop of Ireland

It must be wonderful to be a saint as popular as Saint Patrick is!

Everyone loves St. Patrick! Oh, of course, the Irish claim him because he's their own very special protector. When his feast day, March 17th, comes along, everyone joins in the fun.

There are parties, and dancing, and singing. There is a big parade down Fifth Avenue in New York. Everybody celebrates on St. Patrick's Day!

Practically everyone wears a shamrock. Shamrocks grow in Ireland. They are shipped all over the world in time for the "Big Day."

Nothing much is known about Saint Patrick's birthplace nor his early life, but many tales have come down to us about his later life.

When his was sixteen, things really began to happen! He was captured by pirates and taken to Ireland. Patrick was sold to a cruel pagan named Milcho.

Patrick was too young to do very hard work. "You take care of my sheep herds," ordered Milcho.

What Milcho thought would be a punishment was just what Patrick liked. Here was his chance to pray. Patrick loved to pray. Out in the open fields, while tending the sheep, he felt very close to God.

Six years later, Patrick escaped. He went to live in France with his uncle, the great St. Martin of Tours. Patrick wanted to be a priest, so that he could return to Ireland and teach the little children about Jesus. He spent much of his time studying the Scriptures.

After he was ordained a priest, Patrick prayed that the Pope would send him to Ireland. What a wonderful surprise was in store for Patrick! Not only was he sent back, but, shortly after, he was appointed Bishop of Ireland.

Soon after he returned, the annual celebration took place. All the pagan chiefs met at the king's castle on Tara Hill. Once a year, at the same time as the Christian Easter, the king lighted a big fire there.

At this same time, the different tribes gathered on other hills. No one dared light a fire until the king set up his big flare on Tara Hill.

Now, it just happened that Patrick was celebrating the Easter vigil for his Christians. He blessed and lighted the Easter fire.

Seeing the flame in the distance, the king and his pagan followers could hardly believe their eyes. "Who dares to disobey my orders?" shouted the king. "Go and bring him to me!"

Patrick wasn't the least bit frightened when he was brought before the fierce-looking king.

The king was so furiously angry when he saw how calm Patrick was, that he could only shout, "Who are you? Who are you?"

Before Patrick got a chance to answer him, a few of the pagan priests took the king aside.

"Be careful, O king," they pleaded. "This stranger teaches a new doctrine. Many people believe in him. He has great power."

Patrick wondered why the king looked so frightened. Approaching him, he said, "I am Patrick, a Bishop of the Holy Catholic Church. Pope Celestine has sent me here to teach the people of Ireland about the one, true God."

The pagan priests interrupted again to tell the king some of the wonderful things they had heard that Patrick did. The king was astonished. Fear and anger disappeared. He said, "You do greater things than our pagan gods do. We would like to know more about your God."

Patrick was just waiting for this chance. All of his life he had wanted to tell people about Jesus.

He was so kind and sincere, that it wasn't long before the king said, "You may travel all over Ireland, Patrick. Tell our people all about the one, true God."

So Patrick hurried off. Sure enough, every place he went the people loved him. They listened carefully when he taught them.

It wasn't so easy, though. The pagan magicians were furiously angry, because Patrick had their heathen temples torn down and he erected churches in place of them. The magicians gave Patrick plenty of trouble.

Now, for the part about the shamrock. You have to admit that the Blessed Trinity is hard to explain. Of course, none of us will understand it, not even in heaven. Patrick was really having a hard time explaining this mystery.

Once he happened to look down. "Ah, just the thing!" said Patrick, as he picked a shamrock. "Now you will see what I mean! See these three leaves," he explained. "They are all on one stem, aren't they?" All the people agreed. "Now," said Patrick, "this little green shamrock is a good example of what I am teaching you. Just as these are three leaves on one stem, so are there three Persons in one God."

That is why the shamrock makes Irish people think of the Blessed Trinity.

Some people say that Saint Patrick drove all the snakes out of Ireland. When you see his picture, you see the snakes running away from him in all directions. But there weren't real snakes in Ireland. The story just means that one by one, Patrick did away with all the evil customs that the pagans had started. Most of the pagans became Christians.

Now you can see why Patrick is such a very popular saint, especially with the Irish people.

The next time St. Patrick's Day comes around, don't forget to wear your shamrock and join in the fun.

Saint Elizabeth of Hungary

This is not a fairy tale. It is the story of a real princess who lived in a real castle in Hungary a long, long time ago.

Elizabeth was her name. She was a very happy little girl with beautiful dark curly hair. She was just four years old at the time our story begins.

Elizabeth had so much fun! She was the favorite of everyone in the castle. Even the brave knights who served her father, King Andrew, were very fond of her.

Sometimes her favorite knight would ride over to where Elizabeth was playing, pick her up and gallop away like the wind. He would put his big plumed cap on her tiny head. Everyone would laugh and clap as they galloped away.

One day there was so much excitement in the castle that Elizabeth was frightened. Everyone was rushing around making preparations for important visitors. King Andrew was dashing about giving orders to his servants.

The queen was telling the maids how Elizabeth was to be dressed. Elizabeth didn't like it at all. "How can I run and play, Mother," she said, "with all these stiff clothes on me?" The heavy jewelled bracelets and rings were beautiful, but Elizabeth was hoping important visitors wouldn't come to the castle often.

Poor little princess! The visitors had come from Thuringia, a province in Germany, to take her back with them.

She was going to live in the Wartburg Castle. Her parents had promised her in marriage to Prince Louis, who was six years older than Elizabeth. Louis was a noble prince. He loved Elizabeth and watched over her as though she were his little sister.

Elizabeth had to learn the duties of a ruler's wife, so that she could help Louis after they grew up and were married.

How Elizabeth missed her parents and her friends! Her new home was a dark and gloomy castle. It frightened her to walk through the long dark halls. There were so many ugly pillars and staircases! It was very easy to get lost in this spooky place.

Prince Louis' mother was very kind to Elizabeth, but oh, it was so hard for the little girl to remember all the things she must do. "Stand up straight, Elizabeth!" "Don't run, Elizabeth!" "A princess must never shout, Elizabeth!" "Don't do this, Elizabeth!" "Don't do that, Elizabeth!" It was dreadful for the once happy princess.

Louis had a sister, Agnes. She was mean and jealous. She didn't like the little girl who would some day rule over Thuringia with Louis.

Often, when they were playing games, Elizabeth would suddenly run away to visit Jesus in the castle chapel.

"Elizabeth thinks she's so holy!" Agnes would complain. "She can't even play without stopping to talk to beggars or to run to church. Church is only for Sundays, anyway!" she would say.

Time passed quickly. Then the wedding day came. Elizabeth looked lovely in her white satin wedding gown trimmed with lace. Her cape was of white velvet adorned with solid gold braid. On her wavy hair was a tiny tiara of sparkling diamonds. Louis felt that he had the most beautiful bride in all the world!

Louis, in blue satin, with a gold crown on his head, looked handsome. They were so happy! They rode in a beautiful coach. Noble knights, on prancing white horses, rode in the cavalcade. The wedding and feasting were soon over.

Elizabeth and Louis attended daily Mass in the castle chapel. Louis would then go about his duties. Elizabeth spent her days in prayer and in looking after the needs of the poor and sick of the town below the castle hill.

Agnes often complained to Louis. "Elizabeth acts like a servant!" she would say. "She doesn't act like a princess at all; she gives everything away to the poor!"

Louis paid no attention. He loved his wife dearly, and he knew she was very holy. However, he did forbid her to carry heavy loads on her errands to the poor.

One day, when he met her trudging along the road carrying something very heavy under her cloak, he became angry and he cried, "Elizabeth, what are you carrying?"

With a sweet smile on her face, Elizabeth opened her cloak. Within its folds were the most beautiful red roses Louis had ever seen. God had performed a miracle to show Louis that He was pleased with Elizabeth's love for the poor.

Do you know what Louis did? He knelt right down there in the road and kissed Elizabeth's hand. He loved her more than ever after that.

Six years after they were married, Louis went off to war as a Crusader. Elizabeth was proud of her soldier husband, yet her heart was broken. She felt that he would never return. But her three lively little children kept her very busy during the long days without Louis.

One day the dreaded message came. Louis had sent her his ring. This was his way of letting her know that the message was really from him. He had been very ill. Just before he had died, he had given the ring to one of his loyal men to bring to his dear wife.

Elizabeth was very sad and lonely without her loving husband.

Louis' jealous family made Elizabeth so unhappy that she sent her children away to a boarding school. She gave all her own money to the poor. She went to live alone in a small house. God blessed her work among the poor of the village. Sometimes Our Lady appeared to her to give her comfort.

For the love of God, Elizabeth spent the rest of her life serving the sick and the poor peasant people in Thuringia.

When she died, everyone in Thuringia was sad. They loved and admired Elizabeth. Even the Emperor of Germany came to her funeral. They knew in their hearts that she was a saint.

The emperor did a wonderful thing! He took the golden crown off his head, and placed it on Elizabeth's.

"She is indeed a queen," said the emperor. "She deserves a crown!"

After her death, many people prayed to her and asked her help as they had during her lifetime.

Four years later the Pope proclaimed Elizabeth a saint. Her feast day is celebrated on November 17th.

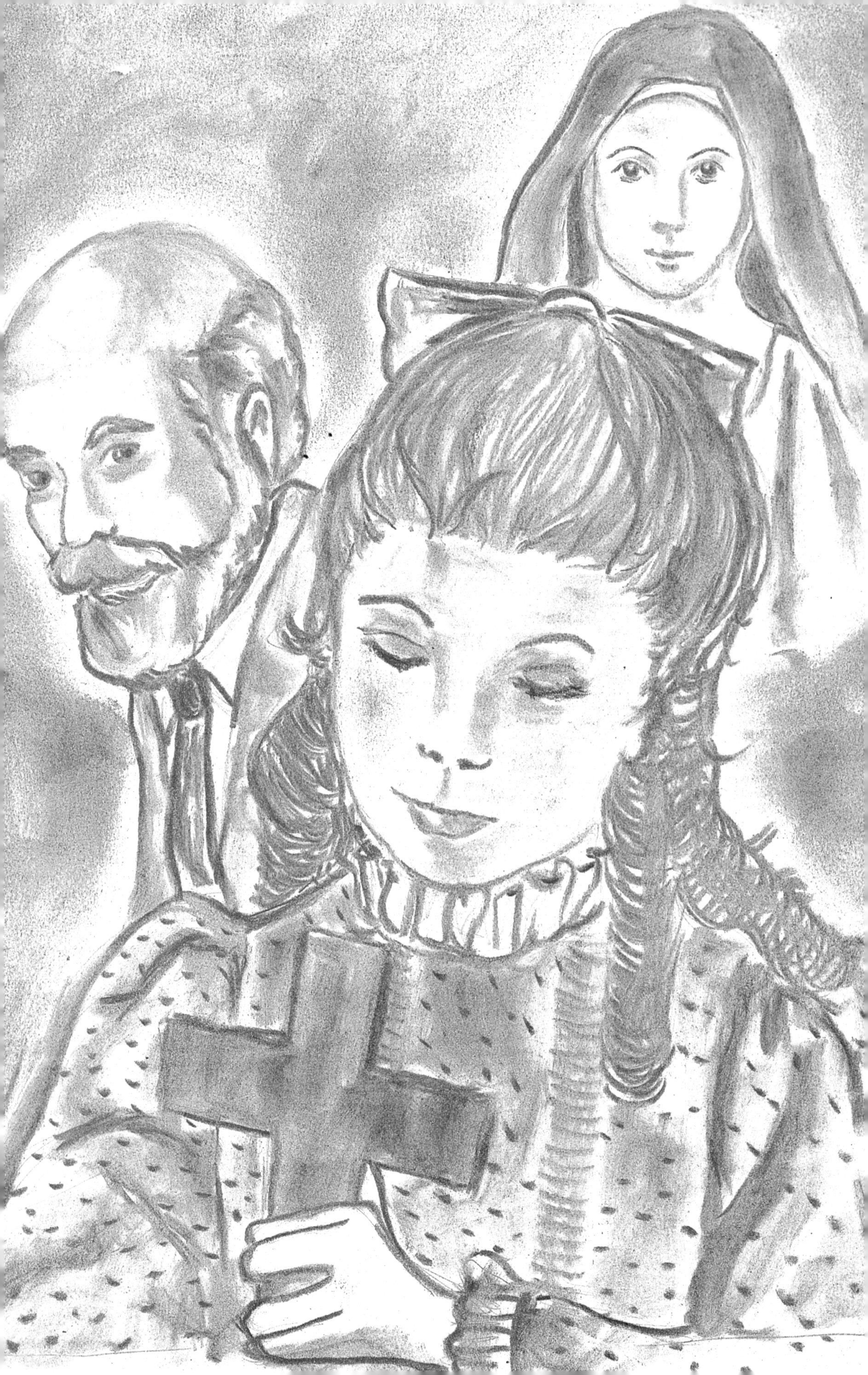

Saint Therese of Lisieux

Not so many years ago, there lived in France a very happy family by the name of Martin.

At the time our story begins, there was a lot of excitement going on in the Martin home.

There was a new baby. She was beautiful! Her name was Therese.

Monsieur and Madame Martin were very loving parents. They were so proud of their five lovely girls! There was Marie, who was thirteen. Then, there were Pauline, Leonie, Celine, and the baby, Therese.

"The Little Queen," as her father loved to call Therese, grew to be a lovely child. Her large blue eyes twinkled with mischief. Her golden hair was beautiful. As she scampered around the house and garden, she gave joy to everyone who met her.

Celine, who was three years older, was Therese's playmate. They were always together!

One day Leonie was busy packing her suitcase. She had begged her parents to send her to boarding school. At last she was going! It would be wonderful there! It would be so much more fun than having lessons at home!

Leonie felt very grown-up indeed. "I must get rid of all these baby things," she said. "I'm too old for them now." She put all her dolls, doll clothes, toys, and trinkets into a big clothes basket.

"Come, Celine; come, Therese," Leonie called, as she carried her heavy load into the playroom. "See all these beautiful things! They are all for you!"

"For us?" they cried. Oh! They could hardly believe their eyes.

"Come, Celine," said Leonie, "you take first choice." Celine was so overcome with all this sudden wealth that she just stood looking at it. It was all so beautiful! How hard it was to choose!

Timidly, she chose a piece of brightly colored silk. "For my doll," she said.

There was nothing timid about Therese's choice. Standing on tiptoe and reaching up, she grabbed the whole basketful—dolls, doll clothes, colorful balls—all of it. "I choose everything!" she cried. Then, stumbling under the load, she hurried from the room, fearing that Leonie might change her mind.

All her life Therese really did choose everything. God sent her not only joys, but sorrows also. She took everything He sent, whether it was pleasant or unpleasant, just as cheerfully as she had taken the basket of treasures.

When Therese was four, God took her lovely mother to heaven. Her sister, Pauline, became her "special mother."

Therese was the constant companion of her father. They had so much fun together! They went fishing, and on picnics. One day Therese said to Pauline, "I hope the great men of Paris don't find out how wise Papa is. They would surely make him king. Then France would have all its problems solved! But I'd lose Papa."

On Sunday evenings, after Vespers in Church, Therese and her father would walk home together. Sometimes Therese would say, "Papa, lead me!" Then, with her little hand in his large one, she would walk along looking up at the stars. One evening, they seemed to be brighter than ever. "Look! Papa, look!" she cried out, "My name is written in heaven!"

Sure enough, there was Orion, which is a group of stars forming the letter "T." Therese had never noticed it before. She really believed it was placed there by God, just for her.

In Lisieux, there was a Carmelite convent. There, the nuns joyfully served God and prayed for His people. First Pauline and then Marie went to Carmel to join these sisters. Therese could hardly wait until she was old enough to join them.

Finally, the wonderful day came! Therese was very happy! However, she realized that she was very young, and not in good health. She wanted only to please Jesus. Therese decided not to try to find very difficult things to do. She would do the little, everyday things in the best way she could. She called this her "Little Way to Holiness."

You and I can easily imitate her "Little Way."

When Therese became very ill, after only nine years in Carmel, do you know what she said? "From the age of three, I have always said 'Yes' to God." That was her way of loving Jesus.

So let us tell Saint Therese that we want to practice her "Little Way." She will ask God to help us. And I am sure of what His answer will be. He will say "Yes" to Therese.

ALSO AVAILABLE FROM ST. PAUL EDITIONS

The Fisher Prince

Daughters of St. Paul
St. Peter, fisherman and apostle, the Rock of Christ's Church.
EN0090

The Great Hero

Daughters of St. Paul
St. Paul the Apostle—adventures of the greatest among the pioneers and saints.
EN0150

Footsteps of a Giant

Daughters of St. Paul
Charles Borromeo's tireless labor during the Council of Trent continued afterwards in fidelity to reform, to change of heart and conduct in the flock entrusted to him.
EN0110

No Place for Defeat

Daughters of St. Paul
Pius V, the Pope who was a Dominican monk, renowned for his orthodoxy, his courage and mildness.
EN0220

A Brief Catholic Dictionary For Young People

Daughters of St. Paul
This handy pamphlet-dictionary defines simply and clearly the words most often used in religious education today.
CH0125

Daughters of St. Paul

MASSACHUSETTS
50 St. Paul's Ave., Jamaica Plain, Boston, MA 02130 **617-522-8911.**
172 Tremont Street, Boston, MA 02111 **617-426-5464; 617-426-4230.**

NEW YORK
78 Fort Place, Staten Island, NY 10301 **718-447-5071; 718-447-5086.**
59 East 43rd Street, New York, NY 10017 **212-986-7580.**
625 East 187th Street, Bronx, NY 10458 **212-584-0440.**
525 Main Street, Buffalo, NY 14203 **716-847-6044.**

NEW JERSEY
Hudson Mall Route 440 and Communipaw Ave.,
Jersey City, NJ 07304 **201-433-7740.**

CONNECTICUT
202 Fairfield Ave., Bridgeport, CT 06604 **203-335-9913.**

OHIO
2105 Ontario Street (at Prospect Ave.), Cleveland, OH 44115 **216-621-9427.**
616 Walnut Street, Cincinnati, OH 45202 **513-421-5733.**

PENNSYLVANIA
1719 Chestnut Street, Philadelphia, PA 19103 **215-568-2638; 215-864-0991.**

VIRGINIA
1025 King Street, Alexandria, VA 22314 **703-549-3806.**

SOUTH CAROLINA
243 King Street, Charleston, SC 29401 **803-577-0175.**

FLORIDA
2700 Biscayne Blvd., Miami, FL 33137 **305-573-1618.**

LOUISIANA
4403 Veterans Memorial Blvd. Metairie, LA 70006 **504-887-7631; 504-887-0113.**
423 Main Street, Baton Rouge, LA 70802 **504-336-1504; 504-381-9485.**

MISSOURI
1001 Pine Street (at North 10th), St. Louis, MO 63101 **314-621-0346.**

ILLINOIS
172 North Michigan Ave., Chicago, IL 60601 **312-346-4228; 312-346-3240.**

TEXAS
114 Main Plaza, San Antonio, TX 78205 **512-224-8101.**

CALIFORNIA
1570 Fifth Ave. (at Cedar Street), San Diego, CA 92101 **619-232-1442.**
46 Geary Street, San Francisco, CA 94108 **415-781-5180.**

WASHINGTON
2301 Second Ave. (at Bell), Seattle, WA 98121 **206-441-3300.**

HAWAII
1143 Bishop Street, Honolulu, HI 96813 **808-521-2731.**

ALASKA
750 West 5th Ave., Anchorage, AK 99501 **907-272-8183.**

CANADA
3022 Dufferin Street, Toronto 395, Ontario, Canada.